THE
100 CALORIE
BOOK*

*How to eat
only 100 calories worth of
anything you want

BY
Lawrence Sloan
and
Charles Gates

PRICE/STERN/SLOAN
Publishers, Inc., Los Angeles
1981

This book is meant to be a general guide to foods containing approximately 100 calories. The publisher, of course, cannot assume responsibility for differences in the caloric content of processed foods since these vary between manufacturers. This book is not intended to be followed as a diet program. Always see your doctor before starting any weight reduction program.

Copyright© 1981 by Price/Stern/Sloan Publishers, Inc.
Published by Price/Stern/Sloan Publishers, Inc.
410 North La Cienega Boulevard, Los Angeles, California 90048

ISBN: 0-8431-0332-9

It's not what you eat, it's how much!

Whether you're trying to shed a few pounds or maintain your fabulous physique, you're careful about the foods you eat. However, when hunger strikes it's tough to say "no" to your favorite snacks.

Fear not! THE 100 CALORIE BOOK is your answer. You'll find hundreds of foods listed to help you fight fat and have fun doing it! Now you can nibble on some pizza, taste a piece of pie or slowly sip on ¼ of a milkshake. All your best-loved foods are listed in portions of approximately 100 calories each.

The calorie compositions of foods vary. Differences in portion size, variances in manufacturer's ingredients, and even the conditions under which fresh food is grown can modify its basic caloric content. This book is a general guide to foods apportioned to approximately 100 calories. Use it as a guide to your eating and snacking. You're sure to find some exciting and unusual snacking surprises.

HAPPY MUNCHING!

From Soup
. . .to Nuts

from soup
...to nuts

SOUP	amount	size
Alphabet Soup Mix (Golden Grain)	14½	oz.
Bean and Ham (Campbell)	⅓	can
Beef (Campbell)	1¼	cups
Beef Cup-A-Soup (Lipton)	1½	cups
Beef Noodle (Manischewitz)	1⅓	cups
Beef or Chicken bouillon	14	cubes
Bird's Nest	1	large bowl
Cheddar Cheese (Campbell)	½	cup
Chicken 'N' Dumplings (Campbell)	1	cup
Chicken 'N' Rice (Ann Page)	2	cups
Clam Chowder (Howard Johnson)	½	cup
Cream of Celery (Ann Page)	1½	cups
Lentil (Progresso)	5	oz.
Lobster Bisque	½	cup
Minestrone (Crosse & Blackwell)	½	cup
Mushroom (Campbell)	1¼	cups
Onion Cup-A-Soup (Lipton)	2¼	cups
Oyster Stew (Campbell)	1¾	cups
Split Pea	½	cup
Tomato (Campbell)	1¼	cups
Tomato with Rice (Manischewitz)	1¼	cups
Vegetable, condensed (Campbell)	1¼	cups
Vegetable Mix (Lipton Lite Lunch)	½	pkg.
Vichyssoise (Crosse & Blackwell)	¾	can
Won Ton (Mow Sang)	7	oz.

from soup ...to nuts

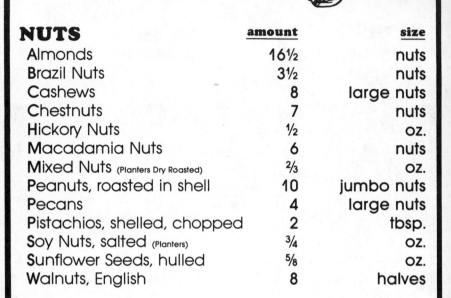

NUTS	amount	size
Almonds	16½	nuts
Brazil Nuts	3½	nuts
Cashews	8	large nuts
Chestnuts	7	nuts
Hickory Nuts	½	oz.
Macadamia Nuts	6	nuts
Mixed Nuts (Planters Dry Roasted)	⅔	oz.
Peanuts, roasted in shell	10	jumbo nuts
Pecans	4	large nuts
Pistachios, shelled, chopped	2	tbsp.
Soy Nuts, salted (Planters)	¾	oz.
Sunflower Seeds, hulled	⅝	oz.
Walnuts, English	8	halves

Fruits and Vegetables

fruits and vegetables

FRUITS	amount	size
Apples (without worm)	1	medium
Applesauce, unsweetened	1	cup
Apricots	6	medium
Avocados	¼	average
Bananas	1	medium
Banana Flakes, dehydrated	1	oz.
Blueberries, fresh	1	cup
Cantaloupes	1	medium
Cherries	½	pound
Cranberries	½	pound
Figs, dried	2	figs
Figs, raw	2	medium
Grapes	5½	grapes
Grapefruits	1	small
Guavas	2	small
Kumquats	8⅓	kumquats
Lemons, peeled	5	average
Oranges, navel	2	medium
Peaches	3	medium
Pears	1	average
Pineapples, fresh trimmed	6.8	oz.
Plumbs, damson	15	small
Plumbs, Japanese and hybrid	2½	average
Prunes	5	large
Quinces, whole	10	oz.
Raisins	1	oz.
Raspberries, black	1	cup
Strawberries, fresh	10	oz.
Watermelon	1	10"x2" slice

fruits and vegetables

FRUIT JUICES	amount	size
Apple	6	oz.
Blackberry	1	cup
Apricot Nectar	6	oz.
Cranberry	½	cup
Grape	½	cup
Grapefruit, fresh	1	cup
Grapefruit, canned, sweetened	6	oz.
Lemon	25	tbsp.
Lime Juice	24	tbsp.
Orange, fresh	1	cup
Orange, Frozen concentrate	1	cup
Pineapple	5	oz.
Prune	4	oz.
Tomato	2	cups
V-8 (Campbell)	3	6 oz. cans

VEGETABLES		
Artichokes, raw	18	small
Asparagus Spears, boiled	32	spears
Beans, fresh green, boiled	1	pound
Beans, lima, cooked or canned	½	cup
Bean Sprouts, raw	3	cups
Beets, fresh, boiled	6	medium
Broccoli, raw	18	oz.
Broccoli Spears, frozen	2	cups
Brussels Sprouts	12½	sprouts
Cabbage	1	pound
Carrots	7	average

fruits and vegetables

	amount	size
Cauliflower	2	pounds
Celery	13	large stalks
Chinese Vegetables, canned	5	cups
Cucumbers, with skin	1½	pounds
Eggplant, cooked, boiled	2½	cups
Endive	12	heads
Endive Leaves	200	small
Kohlrabi, cooked	2½	cups
Leeks	6	average
Lettuce, iceberg	1½	heads
Lettuce, Boston	4	heads
Lettuce, romaine	60	8" leaves
Mushrooms, chopped	5	cups
Parsley	25	sprigs
Parsnips, boiled	1	whole (9"X2¼" size)
Peas, fresh boiled	5	oz.
Peas, frozen	1	cup
Peas and Carrots, frozen	1½	cups
POTATOES		
Baked, peeled	1	average
Boiled	1	average
French-fried strips	5	strips
Mashed, milk added	⅔	cup
Sweet, baked in skin	3	oz.
Radishes	57	small
Spinach, raw, whole	18.8	oz.
Squash, summer	18	average
Shallots	50	cloves
Tomatoes, regular	3	medium
Tomatoes, cherry	7	medium
Tofu	5	oz.
Zucchini	22	oz.

Meat, Fish and Poultry

meat, fish and poultry

MEAT, FISH AND POULTRY	amount	size
Abalone, raw	3.6	oz.
Bacon	3	thin strips
Barracuda, raw	3	oz.
Bass, raw	8	oz.
BEEF		
Ground, broiled	1½	oz.
Hearts	2	1 oz. slices
Roast (Arby's Sandwich)	½	junior size
Sliced, in barbecue sauce (Banquet Buffet Supper)	⅓	8 oz. pkg.
Stew, canned (Armour Star)	½	cup
Stew, homemade	½	cup
Bologna (Oscar Mayer)	1½	slices
Bonito, raw	2	oz.
Brains, raw	2.8	oz.
CHICKEN		
Broiled, no skin	3	oz.
Chow Mein, canned	1	cup
Drumstick, fried	1	2 oz. portion
Pot Pie, frozen (Swanson's)	1/5	8 oz. pkg.
Livers, simmered	2½	pieces
Ribs	2½	ribs
Clams, meat only	2	cups
Cod, raw	4.5	oz.
Crab, steamed in shell	½	pound
Duck, raw	2	1 oz. slices
Enchiladas, canned, gravy (El Paso)	1	piece
Frankfurters (Oscar Mayer Little Wieners)	3	2" pieces
Hamburger (McDonald's Quarter Pounder)	¼	serving
Ham, boiled (Hormel)	3	1 oz. slices

meat, fish and poultry

	amount	size
Lamb, leg, braised	2	lean 1 oz. slices
Lobster Tail, frozen	1	average piece
Lox	2	oz.
Mexican Dinner, frozen (Swanson 3-Course)	1/6	pkg.
Oysters, raw, Eastern	10	medium
Pate de foie gras	5½	tsp.
Peppers, stuffed, homemade	⅓	serving
Perch, raw, yellow	¼	pound
Pigs Feet, pickled	2	oz.
Quail, ready-to-cook	2.3	oz.
Raviolis, canned, beef (Chef Boy-Ar-Dee)	½	cup
Salami, dry	2	thin slices
Sardines, canned, tomato sauce	1	large
Sausages, link	1½	pieces
Scallops, raw	4	oz.
Scallops, fried	3	small pieces
Shrimp, canned (Bumble Bee)	1	can (4½ oz.)
Shrimp Puff (Durkee)	2	pieces

TUNA

	amount	size
Oil-packed (Bumble Bee)	⅓	6 oz. can
Salad, homemade	2	oz.
Water-packed (Star Kist)	½	7 oz. can

TURKEY

	amount	size
Frozen with gravy (Green Giant Toast Topper)	1	serving (5 oz.)
Roasted, white meat	1½	4"x 2"x ¼" slices
Skinless	1	2 oz. slice
Whale, raw	2½	oz.

sugar 'n' spice

CAKES	amount	size
Brownies, nut, homemade	1	3"x 1"x ⅞" piece
Cakes with frosting, most commercial brands	4	small bites
Cheese Cake, mix (Jell-O)	1/16	8" cake
Cupcakes, plain, 2½" size	1	cupcake
Gingerbread (Dromedary)	1"x 4"	square
Ho-Ho's (Hostess)	1	Ho-Ho
Twinkies (Hostess)	⅔	piece

CANDY	amount	size
Almond Joy Bar	1	section
Baby Ruth Bar	¾	oz.
Bit-O-Honey	3	pieces
Breath Mints (Certs)	12½	pieces
Butterscotch Morsels (Nestle's)	41	pieces
Caramels (Kraft)	3	pieces

CHOCOLATE	amount	size
Covered Ants	4	ants
Covered Cherries (Brach's)	1½	cherries
Covered Raisins (Nabisco)	25	pieces
Hershey's Bar	⅔	bar
Fudge, homemade	1"	square
Gum Drops	1	oz.
Ju Jus	15	pieces
Jujifruit	12	pieces
Licorice, black	1	oz.
Life Savers, peppermint	14⅓	pieces
M & M's, plain	⅔	oz.
M & M's, peanut	⅔	oz.
Milky Way	1	8 oz. bar
Mounds Bar	1	section

sugar 'n' spice

	amount	size
Sugar Babies	15	pieces
Toffies (Rothchild's)	4½	pieces
Tootsie Rolls, midget size	3⅞	pieces

COOKIES

	amount	size
Animal Crackers (Nabisco)	9	animals
Chocolate Chip (Chips Ahoy!)	2	cookies
Cream-filled Cookies (Oreo)	2	cookies
Fortune Cookies (Chun King)	3	cookies & fortune
Graham Crackers (Sunshine)	6	crackers
Gingersnaps	5	average snaps
Macaroons (Nabisco Bake Shop)	1	cookie
Oatmeal (Pepperidge Farm)	2	cookies
Peanut Butter Patties (Sunshine)	3⅓	cookies
Raisin Biscuit (Nabisco)	2	cookies
Wafers (Nabisco)	3	cookies
Wafers, vanilla (Sunshine)	7	cookies
Zwiebach Crackers	3⅓	crackers

GUM

	amount	size
Adams Sour	10	sticks
Bubble Gum (Bazooka)	3	3¢ pieces
Chicklets	16	pieces
Dentyne	20	sticks
Doublemint	12½	sticks
Juicy Fruit	12¼	sticks

ICE CREAM

	amount	size
Bar, chocolate-covered (Sealtest)	½	2½ oz. bar
Cones, empty	5	average
Dished	6¼	tbsp.
Sandwich (Sealtest)	2	oz.
Ice Milk	½	cup
Ice Pops, twin stick (Sealtest)	4	oz.

sugar 'n' spice 'n'...

	amount	size
Italian Ices	1	scoop
Milkshakes, chocolate (McDonald's)	¼	container
Milkshakes, vanilla (McDonald's)	⅓	container
Sherbert	6	tbsp.

PUDDING AND PIE

	amount	size
Apple Pie (Drakes)	½	2 oz. pie
Banana Cream Pie, frozen (Morton's)	1/12	16 oz. pie
Banana Pudding (Royal)	¼	cup
Boston Cream Pie, homemade	1/24	8" pie
Butterscotch Pudding (Jell-O)	¼	cup
Cherry, frozen (Morton Mini)	1/6	8 oz. pie
Chocolate Cream Pie, frozen (Morton)	1/12	16 oz. pie
Chocolate Pudding (Jell-O)	¼	cup
Pecan Pie, frozen (Morton Mini)	1/6	6½ oz. pie
Pumpkin Pie, frozen (Banquet)	1/12	20 oz. pie
Vanilla Pudding (Jell-O)	¼	cup

MISCELLANEOUS SNACKS

	amount	size
Corn chips (Fritos)	½	oz.
Custard	⅓	cup
Diet Bars (Pillsbury Food Sticks)	2	sticks
Egg Rolls (Chun King)	3	cocktail size
Fruit Salad, light syrup, canned	¾	cup
Grasshoppers, fried	2	grasshoppers
Gelatin, any flavor (Jell-O)	½	cup
Gelatin, unflavored (Knox)	3½	envelopes
Jam	2	tbsp.
Jelly	2	tbsp.
Marshmallows	4	average
Onion Dip	3½	tbsp.
Peanut Butter	1	tbsp.
Pizza, homemade	1/16	14" pie

snacks that are nice

	amount	size
Pizza Rolls, sausage (Jeno's)	2½	pieces
Popcorn, popped, without butter	4	cups
Popcorn, popped, with butter	2	cups
Poptarts, fruit flavored (Kellogg's)	½	average pastry
Potato Chips (Lay's)	8	chips
Pretzles	6	average
Streudel, frozen (Pepperidge Farm)	1/12	pastry
Tacos, beef (Patio)	2½	cocktail size
Yogurt, vanilla (Dannon)	4	oz.
Sugar, brown, packed	2	tbsp.
Sugar, granulated	6½	tsp.
Sweetner (Weight Watcher's)	5	packets
Quick (Nestle's)	4	heaping tsp.

Breads, Cereals and Grains

breads...

BREADS:	amount	size
Biscuits, prepared (Hungry Jack)	1	biscuit
BREAD VARIETIES:		
Boston Brown	1	slice
Bread Crumbs	20	tbsp.
Cinnamon Toast	½	slice
Date-Nut	1	slice
French	1	slice
Protein	2	slices
White (Weight Watcher's)	3	slices
White (Wonder)	1½	slices
Whole Wheat (Pepperidge Farm)	1½	slices
Breadsticks, plain (Stella D'oro)	2½	sticks
CRACKERS:		
Cheddar Cheese Goldfish	35	pieces
Cheese Nips	17	pieces
Chipsters (Nabisco)	50	pieces
Ritz (Nabisco)	5½	pieces
Salted (Nabisco)	8	pieces
Doughnuts, cake-type	1	⅞ oz. doughnut
Matzo (Manischewitz)	1	sheet
Pancakes (Hungry Jack Extra Light)	2	3½" pancakes
ROLLS:		
Apple (Sara Lee)	1	roll
Cinnamon (Sara Lee)	1	roll
French, sourdough (Francisco)	1	roll
Tortillas, canned (El Paso)	2½	pieces
Tortillas, homemade	1½	pieces
Waffles, homemade	½	7"x 5" waffle
Waffles, prepared, jumbo (Aunt Jemima)	1	waffle

cereals and grains

CEREALS	amount	size
Corn Flakes (Kellogg's)	1	cup
Cream of Wheat	¾	cup
Oatmeal, instant, dry	16	tbsp.
Rice Krispies (Kellogg's)	1	cup
GRAINS		
Farina	1	cup
Flour	1	oz.
Granola	4/5	oz.
RICE:		
Brown, long grain	½	cup
Instant (Uncle Ben's)	½	cup
Rice-A-Roni, chicken or beef	⅓	cup
White, long grain	½	cup
Wheat Germ (Kretschmer)	¼	cup

Pasta and
Noodles

pasta and noodles

	amount	size
Lasagne, frozen (Buitoni)	3	oz.
Lasagne, mix (Chef Boy-Ar-Dee)	3	oz.
MACARONI		
And Cheese, homemade	¼	cup
And Cheese, mix (Golden Grain)	⅛	pkg.
Buttered	½	cup
Plain, tender	⅔	cup
Manicotti, frozen (Buitoni)	1	piece
NOODLES		
And Beef, canned (Heinz)	5	oz.
Buttered	4	oz.
Chow Mein	½	cup
Italiano, mix (Betty Crocker)	¼	cup
Meatballs, sauce, canned (Buitoni)	4	oz.
Plain, cooked	½	cup
Romanoff, mix (Betty Crocker)	⅛	pkg.
Tuna, frozen (Stouffer's)	3	oz.
Noodle-Roni, au gratin	3	oz.
Noodle-Roni, chicken/almonds	⅓	cup
Noodle-Roni, parmesan	⅓	cup
PIZZA		
Frozen, cheese (Celeste)	⅛	7 oz. pie
Homemade, plain	1/16	14" pie
Mix (General Mills Skillet Pizza)	⅛	pkg.
Ravioli, canned (Franco-American)	3¾	oz.
SPAGHETTI		
And Sauce, Casserole, frozen (Morton)	½	pkg.
And Sauce, frozen (Banquet)	1	oz.
Buttered	4	oz.
Plain	½	cup
Spaghetti-O's, canned (Franco-American)	5	oz.

Dairy
Products

dairy products

DAIRY	amount	size
Butter	1	tbsp.
CHEESE		
American	1	oz.
Camembert	1½	oz.
Cottage, creamed	½	cup
Cream (Kraft Philadelphia)	1	oz.
Gruyere	1	oz.
Muenster	1	oz.
Monterey Jack	1	oz.
Parmesan, grated	4	tbsp.
Riccotta	2	oz.
Romano, grated (Frigo)	5	tbsp.
CREAM		
Coffee	3	tbsp.
Half and Half	5	tbsp.
Sour	3	tbsp.
Whipping	2	tbsp.
Eggs	1	large
Egg Nog	⅓	cup
Egg, omelette	1	medium
MILK		
Buttermilk	1	cup
Chocolate	½	cup
Cream, light	3	tbsp.
Goat's	1	cup
Low-Fat	1	cup
Skim	1	cup
Whole	⅔	cup
Yogurt, plain (Dannon)	6	oz.

Savory
Condiments

savory condiments

	amount	size
Anchovy Paste	5	tbsp.
Bacon Bits	14	tsp.
Barbecue Sauce (Cris 'N' Pitts)	7	tbsp.
Catsup (Del Monte)	6	tbsp.
Cherries, Maraschino	12½	cherries
Coconut, grated	1	oz.
Horseradish, prepared (Kraft)	1	quart
Honey	1½	tbsp.
Mayonnaise	1	tbsp.
Mustard, brown	20	tsp.
Mustard, yellow	25	tsp.
Olives, pitted	14	olives
Pickles, kosher dills (Claussen)	14	slices
Pickles, sweet (Del Monte)	7	pickles
Relish	5	tbsp.

SALAD DRESSING

	amount	size
French (Kraft)	1½	tbsp.
Prepared (Miracle Whip)	1½	tbsp.
Roquefort (Kraft)	2	tbsp.
Thousand Islands (Wishbone)	1½	tbsp.
Soy Sauce	20	tbsp.
Steak Sauce (A-1)	6	tbsp.
Tabasco Sauce	25	tsp.
Tartar Sauce	4	tsp.
Teriyaki Sauce (Kikkoman)	6	tbsp.

TOPPINGS

	amount	size
Caramel (Smucker's)	5	tsp.
Chocolate (Hershey's)	2	tbsp.
Marshmallow Cream (Kraft)	3	tbsp.
Whipped (Cool Whip)	5	tbsp.
Vinegar	50	tbsp.
Worcestershire Sauce (Heinz)	9	tbsp.

booze 'n' beverages

NON-ALCOHOLIC BEVERAGES

	amount	size
Club Soda		All you can
Cocoa	1	3 oz. mug

COFFEE

	amount	size
Ground Roasted	50	cups
Instant	25	cups
With 1 T. cream	4	cups
With 1 tsp. sugar	5	cups
Mix, flavored	1¼	cups
Turkish with 1 tsp. sugar	1	cup
Viennese with 1 tsp sugar and 1 T. cream	1	cup
Kool-Aid, any flavor	1	8 oz. glass
Lemonade	1	8 oz. glass

SOFT DRINKS

	amount	size
Coca-Cola	1	8 oz. glass
Cream Soda (Fanta)	1	6 oz. glass
Cherry Soda (Shasta)	1	8 oz. glass
Dr. Pepper	1	8 oz. glass
Ginger Ale (Canada Dry)	1	9 oz. glass
Orange Soda (Crush)	1	7 oz. glass
Pepsi Cola	1	8 oz. glass
Root Beer (Hire's)	1	8 oz. glass
Strawberry Soda (Crush)	1	7 oz. glass
Tom Collins Mix	7	oz.
Tonic Water	10	oz.
Water or Tea		All you can

ALCOHOLIC BEVERAGES

	amount	size
Apricot Sour, canned (Party Tyme)	3	oz.
Bourbon	1	jigger

booze 'n' beverages

	amount	size
Brandy	1	jigger
Daiquiri, canned (Party Tyme)	3	oz.
Gin	1	jigger
Gin and Tonic, canned (Party Tyme)	4	oz.
Irish Whiskey	1	jigger
Martini, canned (Party Tyme)	2½	oz.
Pina Colada, canned (Party Tyme)	3	oz.
Rum	1	jigger
Screwdriver, canned (Party Tyme)	3	oz.
Scotch	1	jigger
Vodka	1	jigger
Vodka Tonic, canned (Party Tyme)	4	oz.

BEER

	amount	size
Budweiser	1	8 oz. glass
Coors	1	8 oz. glass
Grenzquell	1	8 oz. glass
Lite	1	12 oz. glass
Michelob	1	8 oz. glass
Miller's	1	8 oz. glass
Natural Light	1	12 oz. glass
Pabst Blue Ribbon	1	8 oz. glass
Schlitz	1	8 oz. glass
Schlitz Malt Liquor	1	7 oz. glass
Stroh's	1	8 oz. glass

WINE

	amount	size
Burgundy (C. Martini)	3	oz.
Cabernet Sauvignon (Inglenook)	1	5 oz. glass
Chablis (B & G)	1	5 oz. glass
Rose (Inglenook)	4	oz.
Sake	5	½ oz. sake cups
Sherry (Dry Sack)	2½	oz.
Thunderbird Wine (Gallo)	1	big swig (3 oz.)

1OO Calorie Menus

BREAKFAST
* 2" Log Cabin Pancake
* 1 pat butter
* 2 tbsp. Diet Delight Pancake Syrup
* ½ large poached egg
* 6 oz. cup of Maxwell House Coffee

LUNCH
* 1 thin slice bacon
* 1 lettuce leaf
* 2 cherry tomatoes
* 1 thin slice white bread

DINNER
* 3 oz. sole, meat only
* 4 oz. spinach
* ⅛ cup Uncle Ben's Quick Rice

100 Calorie Menus

BREAKFAST
* ¼ medium pink grapefruit
* ½ Quaker Shredded Wheat Biscuit
* ½ cup skim milk
* A pot of tea with 1 tsp. sugar

LUNCH

* Peanut Butter sandwich made with ½ slice Wonder Bread spread with 2 tsp. peanut butter

DINNER

* 1 oz. roast turkey
* ½ Finger roll
* 2 oz. boiled peas without butter

STRAWBERRY SHORTCAKE

* ¼ cup fresh strawberries
* 1″ piece sponge cake
* 1 tbsp. Cool Whip Topping

This book is published by

PRICE/STERN/SLOAN
Publishers, Inc., Los Angeles

publishers of

HOW TO FLATTEN YOUR STOMACH ($1.75)

HOW TO TRIM YOUR HIPS AND
SHAPE YOUR THIGHS ($1.75)

COACH JIM EVERROAD'S
5-MINUTE TOTAL SHAPE UP PROGRAM ($1.75)

SUPER FITNESS ($3.95)

FINGER ACUPRESSURE ($3.95)

and many, many more

They are available wherever books are sold, or may
be ordered directly from the publisher by sending
check or money order for the total amount plus 50 cents
for handling and mailing. For a complete list of titles
send a *stamped, self-addressed envelope* to:

PRICE/STERN/SLOAN *Publishers, Inc.*
410 North La Cienega Boulevard, Los Angeles, California 90048